KALEIDOSCOPE

State Government

Suzanne LeVert

BENCHMARK BOOKS

MARSHALL CAVENDISH
NEW YORK

Benchmark Books
Marshall Cavendish
99 White Plains Road
Tarrytown, NY 10591
www.marshallcavendish.com

© 2004 by Marshall Cavendish Corporation

Library of Congress Cataloging-in-Publication Data

LeVert, Suzanne.
  State government / by Suzanne LeVert.
     p. cm. — (Kaleidoscope)
Summary: An introduction to and overview of the three branches of state
government, looking at the role and function of each.
Includes bibliographical references and index.
  ISBN 0-7614-1596-3
  1. State governments—United States—Juvenile literature. [1. State
governments. 2. United States—Politics and government.] I. Title. II.
Kaleidoscope (Tarrytown, N.Y.)
  JK2408L477 2003
  320.473—dc21
                          2003001902

Photo research by Anne Burns Images

Cover photo: Corbis/Saba Najlah Feanny

The photographs in this book are used with permission and through the courtesy of: *Corbis:* Reuters New Media Inc.,
title page, 11; Robert Lewine, 4; Richard Cummins, 7; Joseph Sohm:Visions of America, 8; Rolf Bruderer, 15; W.
Cody, 16; Philip Gould, 20; LWA-Dann Tardif, 23, 35; AFP, 32, 40; Benjamin Rondel, 39; Larry Lee, 43. *Getty Images:*
Alex Wong, 12; David McNew, 24; Joe Raedle, 28; Jim Bourg, 31. *SuperStock:* 19. *AP Photo:* Harry Cabluck, 36.

Series design by Adam Mietlowski

Printed in Italy

6 5 4 3 2 1

Contents

To Meet the Needs

How many days are there in a school year? How fast can you drive on your state's highways? What kinds of tests do doctors and nurses have to pass in order to hold jobs in your state?

These are just a few of the questions state government must answer for its citizens. Members of the state government make laws and set up programs that affect people's daily lives. They create laws and programs that allow roads and bridges to be built so the state's cities and towns can be connected. Lawmakers also decide the amount of tax people must pay, and they help protect citizen's basic rights.

◀ *Your state government decides how many days you go to school every year.*

Each state is unique. It has its own special qualities and challenges based on its location, its history, and the people who live there. Because of these differences, each state government has its own ways of working. But state governments do share a common goal: to meet the needs of the people, now and in the future.

Each state has its own set of needs and concerns. The people of Wisconsin, for example, must follow the laws created and passed by members of their state government. ▶

We the People

re domestic Tranquility, provide for the common

our Posterity, do ordain and establish this Cons

Article I.

Sec. 1. All legislative Powers herein granted shall be vested in a Congress of the United States, which shall consist of a

Sec. 2. The House of Representatives shall be composed of Members chosen every second Year by the People of the several

Federal, State, and Local

The U.S. Constitution gives state governments the power to create and **administrate** laws and programs. It sets up a **federal** system of government. A federal system divides power and responsibility between two levels of government: the national government (also called the federal government) and state governments. The U.S. Constitution also describes the powers that the federal government has and explains that all other powers belong to the states.

◀ *State governments get their power from the U.S. Constitution. This document sets up how the laws of the land should be made and carried out.*

Other levels of power and responsibility in the states include the county, city, and town governments. These groups have the power to make certain rules and run certain programs that affect people on a local level. For instance, a city or town government is responsible for hiring workers to plow the snow after a winter storm. The federal, state, and local governments try to work together to make life in the United States as productive and safe as possible.

After a heavy snowstorm, who will plow the roads? This is one of the important issues some local governments must decide.

Working Together

Each state has important relationships with both the federal government and the other states. The federal government protects the states from foreign invasion. It also makes sure that each state government continues to have a representative democracy, one that allows the people of the state to elect their own officials. In turn, states must not interfere with the power the federal government has to deal with foreign governments and to create money.

◄ *Printing money is one of the jobs of the federal government.*

State governments must also cooperate with one another. Under a legal policy called **full faith and credit**, all states recognize and respect the others' laws. Marriages, divorces, and child-custody decisions made by one state, for example, will still be legal if the couple involved moves to another state.

State governments make their own laws about marriage, divorce, and other parts of family life.

▶

States also often form connections with each other due to their geographic locations. States located in New England, for instance, often come together to help solve problems common to the area. One of those issues involves the fishing industry that uses the waters off of the Atlantic coast. In the Southwest, which has a very dry climate, states work together to make sure that all communities can get the water they need.

◄ *States that face a common concern often work together to solve it. Some of the New England states decided what rules must be followed when fishing the waters off their coasts.*

States also work together with the federal government on a variety of issues. Health care, welfare, and crime are among the problems that need national cooperation. States may also work with the federal government on a regional basis. Seven states in the West—Arizona, California, Colorado, Nevada, New Mexico, Utah, and Wyoming—have joined with the federal government to make sure that one of the region's most important natural resources, the Colorado River, is used wisely.

The mighty Colorado River begins in Rocky Mountain National Park in Colorado, then flows through the Grand Canyon in Arizona before it reaches the Gulf of Mexico. Recently states have come together to help protect its waters.

Setting up State Government

"We the people of the State of Oregon to the end that Justice be established, order maintained, and liberty perpetuated [continued], do ordain this Constitution. . . ." This is how the **preamble** to Oregon's constitution begins. The people of that state **ratified**, or approved, their constitution in 1857, when the area was still called the Oregon Territory.

◄ *State constitutions set up how the state government will be run. Each state had to create these important documents in order to join the Union.*

Just like the nation as a whole, each state has its own constitution. This document describes the rights of its citizens and how the government should be organized. Among the rights state constitutions guarantee are freedom of speech, freedom of religion, and the rights provided to people accused of a crime. Many state constitutions also set up rules for the way government handles finances and taxes, public health and welfare, and natural resources and highways.

Health care is an important issue state governments must face. ▶

Most states have **amended**, or changed, their constitutions at least once during their histories. Amendments are made to deal with new problems or to correct past mistakes. A state constitution may be amended in several ways. The state **legislature,** or law-making body, may offer a proposed amendment to the people of the state. The people then vote whether or not to make the change official. Or the people may come up with their own amendment and vote on it in a statewide election. Some states have special "constitutional conventions" of lawmakers and concerned citizens. They propose an amendment either to the state's voters or legislature for approval.

◀ *Voting is one of the most important rights an American citizen enjoys. Here, on the left, California governor Gray Davis casts his vote in the March 5, 2002, election.*

The state constitution spreads power among three branches of state government. The executive branch (the governor and his or her staff) enforces the laws. The legislative branch (usually a senate and a house of representatives) creates the laws. The judicial branch (the courts) interprets the laws.

The three branches of state government work together to provide services to citizens. Each branch has its own jobs and duties. ▶

Executive Branch

Enforce State Laws

— Governor

— Executive Officers

Legislative Branch

Create & Enact Laws

— Senators

— Representatives

Judicial Branch

Interpret & Apply Laws

— Supreme Court Justices

— Lower Court Judges

The Executive Branch

The **governor** heads the executive branch. This is the branch responsible for carrying out the state laws and business. Among the governor's duties are preparing the state budget, commanding the state **militia**, calling special meetings of the state legislature, and granting pardons to criminals. Governors also represent their states as **ambassadors**, meeting with other state and national leaders. Another important job of the governor is to encourage businesses to invest in his or her state.

◀ *Florida governor Jeb Bush is the leader of his state. Florida voters first elected him in 1998. Here, he meets with children during a visit to an elementary school.*

Several other state officials aid the governor. The **lieutenant governor** helps the governor with his or her daily activities. The lieutenant governor also takes over if the governor cannot finish his or her term of office. The secretary of state usually oversees state elections and keeps track of official state records. The attorney general is the chief legal officer of the state. He or she gives legal advice to the state's agencies and legislature. The attorney general also helps protect the state's **consumers** and environment.

Another important state official is the **comptroller**. The comptroller, also called the controller, keeps track of the state's money and pays the state's bills. In some states, there is another official, called the treasurer, who shares in these financial duties.

The two top officials in state government are the governor and lieutenant governor. In 1998, Massachusetts voters elected Paul Cellucci as governor and Jane Swift as lieutenant governor.

The Legislative Branch

The legislature is the state's law-making body. It usually is called the general assembly or legislative assembly. Most state legislatures meet every year, while others meet every two years. The men and women elected to the legislature often hold other jobs as well.

◄ *Working with the federal government is an important duty of a state legislature. In 2001, President Bill Clinton addressed the Arkansas legislature.*

All but one state legislature—Nebraska's—is made up of two groups, or houses: the senate and the house of representatives. State senators serve for four years while most state representatives serve for two. The men and women elected to the state senate and house of representatives work together to pass, or **enact**, laws that affect the ways people live and work in the state. They create laws to collect taxes and then to spend the money for the public good. Often the lawmakers also work together in committees that focus on specific areas of government, such as education, public health, and finance.

Learning about your state's government is important. It could be the first step to a future job making the laws that will help improve the lives of the people in your state.

The Judicial Branch

The state judicial branch gets its powers from both its state constitution and the U.S. Constitution. It is responsible for interpreting the state's laws and for settling legal disputes among citizens. It also makes sure that citizens are treated fairly under the law.

There are often several different levels of state courts. The state's highest court is the supreme court. The men and women who sit on this court, called justices, explain the state's laws and make decisions about legal issues. Another level of the state court system is the court of appeals. This court considers decisions made by the lower courts, called trial courts or district courts. The court of appeals sees if the decisions were made fairly.

A judge is in charge of a courtroom. He or she helps settle disputes among citizens.

Most cases begin at the trial-court level. Trial courts decide two different kinds of cases: arguments among citizens about private or business matters (called civil cases) and cases involving criminal acts. Most cities and towns have other lower courts to handle matters such as traffic **violations** and landlord-tenant disputes.

State governments must create laws that help keep busy roads and highways safe. They decide how fast we can drive and where we can park, for example. When a driver breaks a traffic law, sometimes the matter is handled by a lower court.

▶

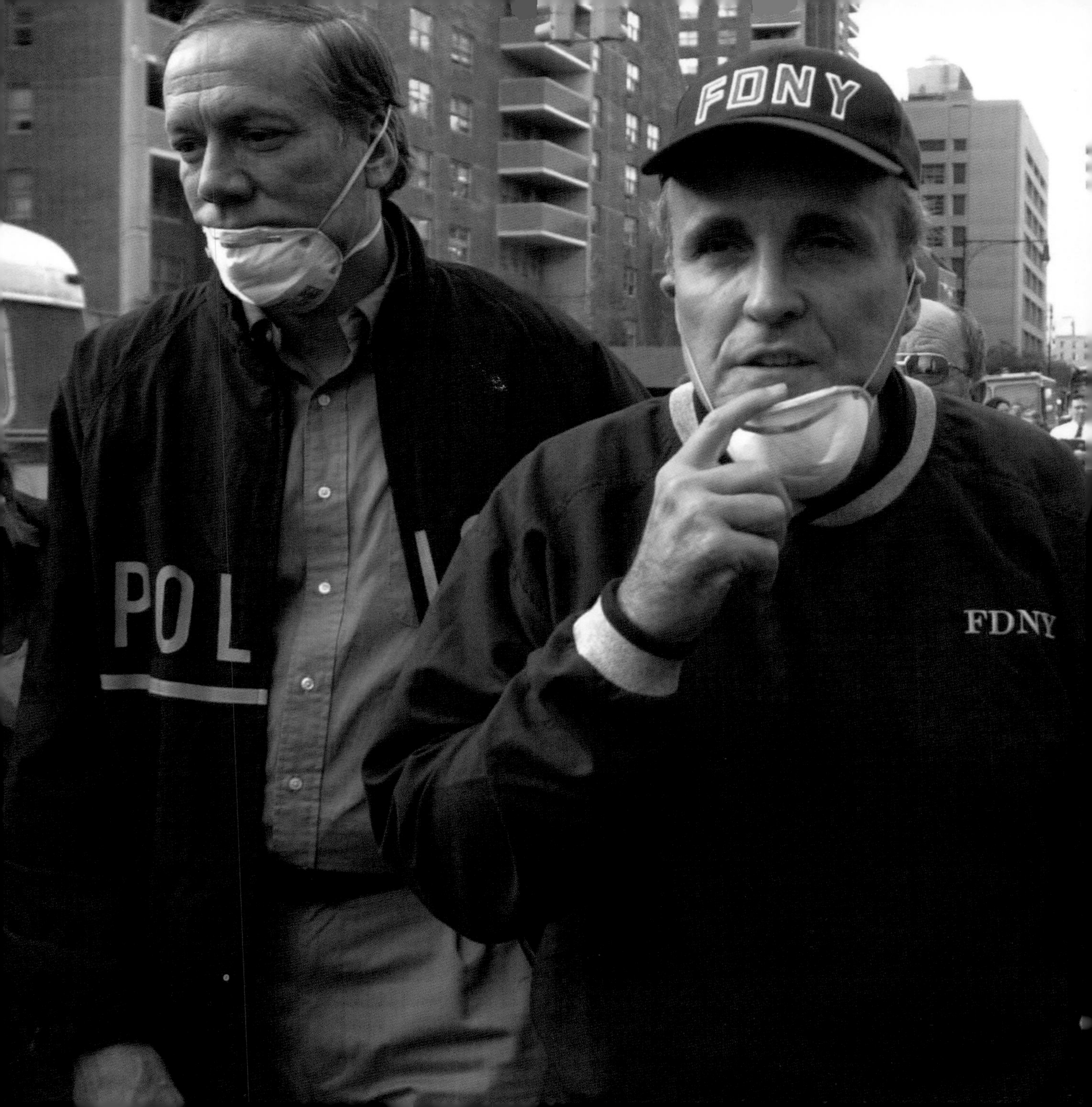

FDNY
POL
FDNY

Facing Future Challenges

As the states look to the future, they face many different challenges. The **terrorist** attacks on September 11, 2001, forced state officials across the country to make sure its citizens are safe. The states also must work to make sure that there are enough jobs for their citizens.

◄ *After the terrorist attacks in 2001, safety is an issue more important than ever. Here, former New York City mayor Rudy Guiliani (right) and New York governor George Pataki (left) visit the site where the World Trade Center buildings once stood.*

The rising costs of health care, the need for better schools, and increasing pollution and other environmental dangers are among the other problems state governments face. Working with local and federal governments and agencies, state governments try to improve the lives of their citizens now and far into the future.

Pollution is a major concern to state governments. Lawmakers work hard to make sure their state's citizens will have a bright future. ▶

Glossary

administrate—Manage or run.

ambassador—A messenger or representative.

amend—To change an existing law or document.

comptroller—A state official who keeps track of the money the state collects in taxes.

consumer—One who buys products or services.

enact—To make into a law.

federal—Relating to the national government of the United States. Also, a system of government that divides power between a national government and state governments.

full faith and credit—The practice of recognizing other states' laws.

governor—The head of the state's executive branch.

legislature—A law-making body of elected representatives.

lieutenant governor—The official who is second in command; the person who takes over the office of governor if the governor cannot serve out his or her term.

militia—A state's military.

preamble—The introduction or beginning.

ratify—Approve by a majority vote.

terrorist—A person who commits a violent act against another group or nation.

violation—When a rule or law is broken.

Find Out More

Books

Harmon, Daniel E. *The Attorney General's Office*. Broomall, PA: Chelsea House, 2001.

Giesecke, Ernestine. *Local Government*. Portsmouth, NH: Heinemann, 2000.

————. *State Government*. Portsmouth, NH: Heinemann, 2000.

Marcovitz, Hal. *The Constitution*. Brookshire, TX: Mason Crest Publishers, 2002.

Marsh, Carole. *The Day That Was Different: September 11, 2001: When Terrorists Attacked America*. Peachtree City, GA: Gallopade, 2001.

Shuker-Haines, Frances. *Rights and Responsibilities: Using Your Freedom*. Austin, TX: Raintree/Steck-Vaughn, 1993.

Web Sites

Government for Kids—State Government
http://www.govspot.com/state/

Great Government for Kids
http://www.cccoe.net/govern/

Learning about the Branches of Government
http://www.kidspoint.org/columns2.asp?column_id=358&column_type=homework

Also, many state government Web sites have a kids' page for the state's youngest citizens. Do a search for your state's official site or have your parents, teacher, or librarian help you.

Author's Bio

Suzanne LeVert is the author of many books for young readers on a host of different topics, including biographies of former Louisiana governor Huey Long and author Edgar Allan Poe. Most recently, she wrote four books in Benchmark Books' Kaleidoscope series on U.S. government, *The Congress, The Constitution, The President,* and *The Supreme Court.*

Index